B is for Beacon

A Great Lakes Lighthouse Alphabet

Written by Helen L. Wilbur and Illustrated by Renée Graef

Known as America's Inland Seas, the Great Lakes, with the rivers, canals, and channels that connect them, form one of the busiest waterways in the world. Native tribes were the original inhabitants on the lakes. The tribes traded furs with Europeans as they came into the area. As European settlement increased, maritime commerce flourished. Lighthouses were needed to secure the safety of ships over the massive freshwater seas.

In 1781 the British established the first light on the Great Lakes at Fort Niagara. After the revolution, the fort and the light became part of the United States.

The first U.S. Congress recognized the importance of lighthouses in developing the new nation. In 1789 it passed a law making the federal government responsible for all lighthouses and beacons.

The Buffalo Main and the Erie Land Lights, established on Lake Erie in 1818, were the first two U.S. lights on the lakes. By the 1860s, that number had jumped to over 70.

A is for America's Inland Seas

The Lakes provided
transportation
and built the heart
of this great nation.

Lighthouses play more than a vital role in navigation; they serve as symbols of courage and loyalty. People are fascinated by lighthouses. Often on remote and beautiful shorelines these magical beacons shine out to warn of danger, offer comfort to travelers on the seas, and lead them to safe harbor.

Early people lit shores with bonfires to direct sailing ships to safety. The first known lighthouse, called the Pharos, stood in Alexandria in Ancient Egypt. Built in the third century BC, it guided ships into the harbor for 1,500 years until it was destroyed in an earthquake.

Before rail, roadways, and air travel, ships were the fastest way to transport people and goods. Lighthouses led ships through treacherous waters to their destinations. Though commercial shipping now uses modern navigational technology, many recreational boaters on the Great Lakes still depend on lighthouses to mark their location.

Lighthouses continue to light the dark and lead us home.

B is for Beacon

Though the voyage is dangerous,
stormy, and long,
the beacon before us
stays steady and strong.

C is for Characteristic

A beacon flashes
from afar
and sailors know
just where they are.

Mariners passing through northern Lake Michigan know immediately when they see the White Shoal Light. Its distinctive spiral candy-cane–painted tower can be seen from miles away and is the only one like it in the U.S. Each lighthouse is painted with a unique color pattern, called a *daymark*, to distinguish it from neighboring lights. Mariners consult light lists and charts to know which lighthouse is in view.

At night the individual flashing pattern and color of a beacon is known as its *characteristic*. The light at Little Sable Point on Lake Michigan is known by its white flash every six seconds.

Foghorns and whistles are used as warnings when visibility is poor. They also have distinct sound patterns. The fog signal at the Cleveland Harbor Main Entrance Light on Lake Erie, locally known as "the cow," had a characteristic of one three-second blast per minute and could be heard from 12 miles away.

Cc

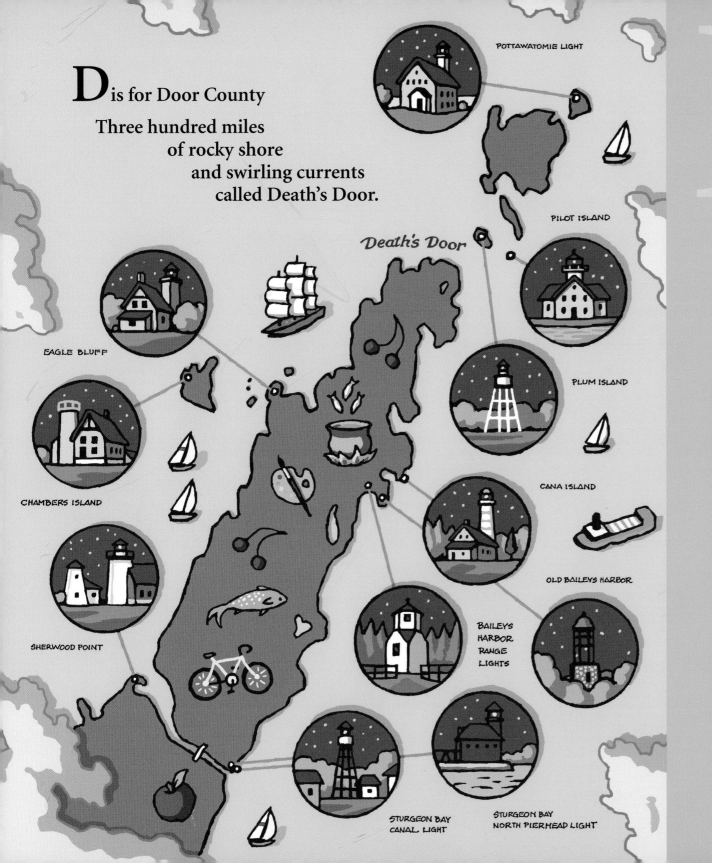

D is for Door County

Three hundred miles
of rocky shore
and swirling currents
called Death's Door.

POTTAWATOMIE LIGHT

Death's Door

PILOT ISLAND

EAGLE BLUFF

PLUM ISLAND

CHAMBERS ISLAND

CANA ISLAND

OLD BAILEYS HARBOR

SHERWOOD POINT

BAILEYS HARBOR RANGE LIGHTS

STURGEON BAY CANAL LIGHT

STURGEON BAY NORTH PIERHEAD LIGHT

Door County rests on a peninsula on Lake Michigan forming the southern entrance to Green Bay. Because of the treacherous waters surrounding it, the first French explorers in the area called it "Port de Morts" or Death's Door. Its 300 miles of rugged coastline are home to 11 lighthouses.

David E. Corbin was the first keeper at the Pottawatomie Lighthouse, built in 1836. He complained of loneliness, having only his horse and dog for company. Despite a special two-week leave to acquire a wife, Corbin died at the light in 1852 still a bachelor.

For 35 years the lighthouse at Eagle Bluff had far merrier occupants in the Duclon family. The Duclons formed a family band and traveled with their instruments, including a piano, to entertain at local events. In winter they loaded everything onto a sleigh.

Visit the Door County Maritime Museum at beautiful Cana Island Lighthouse, then treat yourself to the traditional regional dinner of fish boil and cherry pie.

Because the earth is round, navigational beacons need to be placed high above the earth's surface to be seen from great distances. The higher the elevation of the beam of light, the further away it can shine out to be seen by passing ships.

Split Rock Lighthouse has a yellow brick tower only 54 feet tall, but the light's position on a sheer cliff rising 130 feet over Lake Superior made its beacon visible for 22 miles. Today the lighthouse and its museum attract thousands of tourists each year. When it was built in 1910 that part of Minnesota was wilderness. Crews and materials had to be hoisted from boats at the base of the cliff.

At 113 feet the tallest lighthouse tower in the Great Lakes belongs to the New Presque Isle Lighthouse. You can climb the 144 steps to the top for a great view of the peninsula jutting into Lake Huron.

E is for Elevation

The Split Rock Lighthouse
stands in place
high above
the sheer rock face.

E e

Ff

Every October lighthouse lovers gather in Alpena, Michigan, for the Great Lakes Lighthouse Festival. Four days of events—tours, cruises, exhibits—bring lighthouse fans from all over the country to enjoy themselves, learn about lighthouses, and help preserve these historic buildings.

Communities and organizations on the Great Lakes offer an array of festivals celebrating lighthouses and the area's rich maritime heritage. Among them are:

February
• Great Lakes Shipwreck Festival

June
• Michigan West Coast Lighthouse Festival
• Door County Lighthouse Festival

July
• Toledo Lighthouse Waterfront Festival

September
• Apostle Islands Lighthouse Celebration

October
• Lakeside-Marblehead Lighthouse Festival

Join the celebration. There's something for everyone—boat rides, farmers' markets, crafts, tours, concerts, exhibits, and special activities for kids.

F is for Festivals

Take a tour,
get inspiration;
enjoy a
Great Lakes celebration.

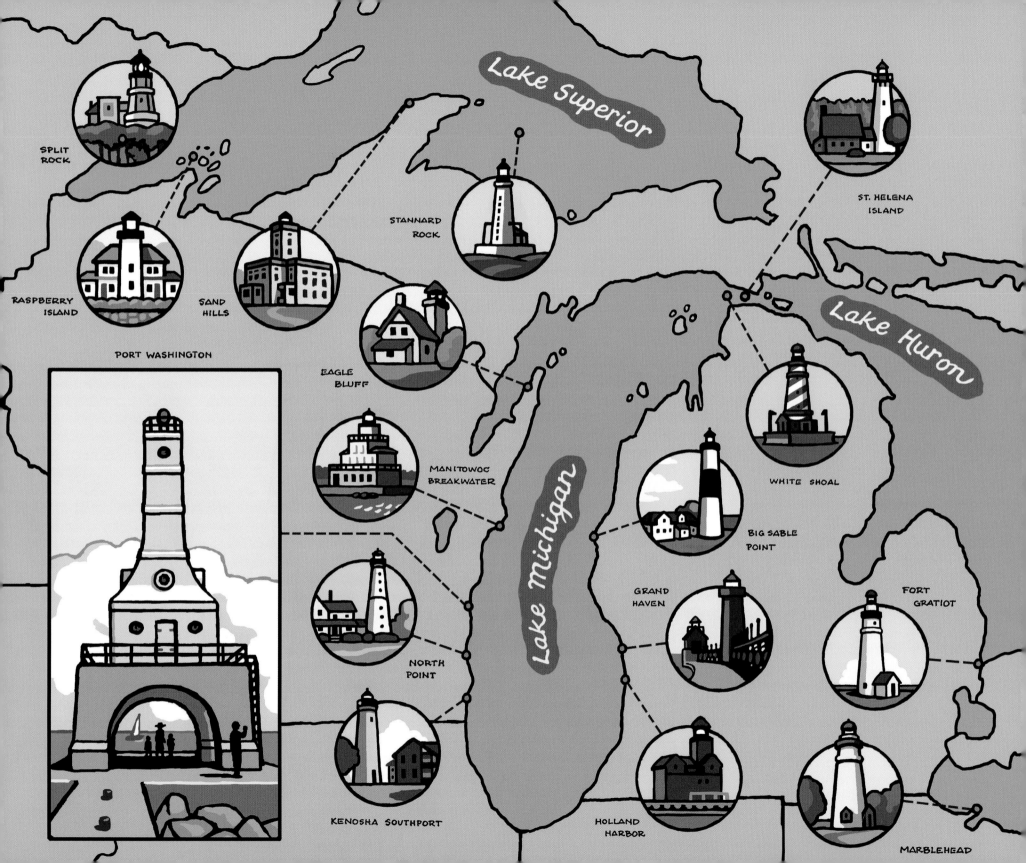

Lake Superior

Lake Huron

Lake Michigan

SPLIT ROCK

RASPBERRY ISLAND

SAND HILLS

PORT WASHINGTON

STANNARD ROCK

EAGLE BLUFF

ST. HELENA ISLAND

MANITOWOC BREAKWATER

WHITE SHOAL

BIG SABLE POINT

NORTH POINT

GRAND HAVEN

FORT GRATIOT

KENOSHA SOUTHPORT

HOLLAND HARBOR

MARBLEHEAD

G is for Great Lakes

From Sunken Rock
to Grand Marais,
the Lakes serve all
for work and play.

BUFFALO MAIN

VERMILLION

Lake Ontario

Lake Erie

BRADDOCK POINT

TIBBETTS POINT

LORAIN WEST

© GRAEF

Formed by glaciers during the last Ice Age, the five Great Lakes make up the largest supply of freshwater in the world. The lakes cover 95,000 square miles of surface area, 10,000 miles of shoreline, and provide drinking water to over 40 million people.

Superior is the largest, deepest, and coldest lake. Huron has the longest shoreline and was the first to be visited by European explorers. Michigan has the world's largest freshwater dune system and is the only lake without a Canadian coastline. Erie is the shallowest and warmest lake with the best walleye pike fishing. Ontario starts at the base of Niagara Falls and its name derives from the native Huron word for shining water.

The Great Lakes form their own ecosystem with thousands of native plants and animals. Bordered by eight U.S. states and Canada, the lakes are home to almost 400 lighthouses (260 on the U.S. side), most of which are still used for navigation for recreational boating as well as commercial shipping.

Gg

H is for Haunted

An eerie presence
chills the air.
You look about
but no one's there.

An isolated spot and a lonely beacon shining into the dark night make a lighthouse the perfect setting for a spooky story.

In 1919, after 47 years on the job, Captain William Robinson died at White River Light Station on Lake Michigan. Visitors still hear footsteps pacing on the upper floor and believe that the captain continues on his nightly rounds, sometimes doing the dusting.

George Parris served as caretaker for the Old Presque Isle Lighthouse on Lake Huron. After George's death in 1992 many have seen an amber beam glowing from the top of the tower even though the Coast Guard had disconnected the light years before.

Perhaps the cutest ghost haunts the Fairport Harbor Lighthouse on Lake Erie. In the 1870s the wife of keeper Captain Joseph Babcock was confined to bed by illness. She was cheered by the antics of her little gray cat whose phantom presence still skitters about the lighthouse like a puff of gray smoke.

Ii

I is for Islands

A speck of green land,
a towering light
guiding our way,
a comforting sight.

There are more than 30,000 islands in the Great Lakes. Some are just big rocks and others are large enough to have towns as well as lakes with islands of their own.

The 22 Apostle Islands in Lake Superior off the coast of northern Wisconsin are known for their lighthouses as well as for their natural beauty. But the first lighthouse in the Apostles got built on the wrong island. In the mid-1800s the boom in fur and lumber shipping called for a light at La Pointe Harbor on Madeline Island. Through some mix-up the contractor built the lighthouse on nearby Michigan Island. In order to get paid he had to build another lighthouse in the right place.

Today the National Park Service manages the Apostle Islands National Lakeshore. The light stations on Michigan Island, Sand Island, Outer Island, Devil's Island, and Raspberry Island are all open to the public and accessible by boat or ferry. A great time to visit is during the Apostle Islands Lighthouse Celebration every September.

Lights and beacons mark man-made as well as natural hazards. Jetties and breakwaters are offshore barriers built to protect harbors. Piers extend into the water to give access to boats and offer pedestrians a pleasant stroll. Lights on these structures help guide vessels into the shelter of a harbor. They tend to be lower since the ships are closer.

Known as "Big Red," the Holland Harbor South Pierhead Light is a familiar landmark and the most photographed lighthouse on Lake Michigan. The Kewaunee Pierhead Light is identical to "Big Red" except that it's white. The buildings are big and square as they once contained huge steam boilers needed to power the enormous horns that produced deafening but lifesaving fog signals.

Some harbors have twin beacons called range lights. Sailors can align the lights one above the other to keep a safe course into a harbor or narrow channel. The St. Joseph Inner and Outer Pier Lights are connected with a narrow catwalk, dangerous in icy conditions but a great subject for winter photography.

Jj

J is for Jetty

The harbor's calm;
    it's a sunny day
but I wish a fish
    would come my way.

K is for Keeper

It's always lit,
every night.
I am the keeper
of the light.

A lighthouse keeper had one charge: keep the light burning. But that mission involved dedication, danger, and countless repetitive tasks on a daily basis. The oil lamps had to be lit from sunset until dawn. During the night the keeper climbed up the tower steps several times to check on the lantern and to wind the mechanism that rotated the light.

During the day the keeper cleaned the lens, polished brass work, repaired and maintained the entire station, its buildings, machinery, and supplies. The lighthouse authorities required a daily log of all activities, weather, and supplies and conducted surprise inspections.

A keeper had to work in the worst weather, putting his or her own life in danger to keep others safe. Keepers were hardy individuals who enjoyed hard work. Two keepers, Willard Cook at the Rock Island Light on Lake Ontario and John Williams at the Waukegan Harbor Lighthouse on Lake Michigan, took on the arduous job despite each having lost an arm in the Civil War.

L is for Lens

Through the prisms,
    a lamp's dim gleam
is made into
    a mighty beam.

Early lighthouses on the Great Lakes burned candles or whale oil to light the lamp. These lamps produced a lot of soot but not much light. In clear conditions the brightest lighthouse could be seen from only 8 to 14 miles away.

In 1822 a French physicist, Augustin-Jean Fresnel, devised a new type of lens that focused all light into an intense beam that could be seen from very far away. A Fresnel lens looks like a giant beehive with rows of glass prisms mounted in a brass frame. The largest size of a Fresnel lens could have more than 1,000 prisms, weigh 4 to 5 tons, and exceed 12 feet in height.

About 16 lighthouses on the Great Lakes still have their original Fresnel lenses in place. You can see them in light stations like the Tibbetts Point Lighthouse on Lake Ontario, the Grosse Pointe Lighthouse on Lake Michigan, or in many of the lakes' maritime museums.

Ll

M is for Michigan

The shifting dunes,
the tall pine trees,
the shores of four
great inland seas.

Which state has the most lighthouses? Michigan has more than 120, making it a top destination for lighthouse lovers. Its 3,288 miles of coastline touch four of the five Great Lakes. With the longest shoreline of any U.S. state except Alaska, Michigan has a rich maritime history.

The oldest Michigan lighthouse, built in 1829, is at Fort Gratiot where the St. Clair River flows into Lake Huron. Recently renovated, the Fort Gratiot Lighthouse stands in a county park open for tours and events.

Michigan takes its maritime heritage seriously. Dozens of nonprofit and volunteer groups work to preserve and maintain lighthouses and their history. The state supports preservation efforts with grants to these groups.

Many Michigan lighthouses, some with adjacent museums, are open to the public. It's a great place to see lighthouses or to stay in one as a volunteer light keeper.

Late November marks the end of the shipping season on the Great Lakes. Ships scramble to make one last run and light keepers prepare to close their stations for the winter. November also brings massive storms with gale-force winds, snow, rain, and towering waves.

Because of their size, the Great Lakes create their own weather system. Arctic air from the north collides with warm Gulf air when a low pressure system sets in. Mariners call the brutal winds that howl across the lakes the "Witch of November."

Many powerful storms have swept across the lakes in November. In 1913 a storm known as the White Hurricane raged for five days, taking over 250 lives and sinking or damaging more than 44 ships.

In winter, ice covers the lakes and the lighthouses. In 1928 a violent storm on Lake Erie encased the Ashtabula Harbor Light in ice. The keepers had to dig through five feet of ice to free themselves.

N n

N is for November

On the lakes
you'd best remember
the howling witch
that stalks November.

O is for Offshore

The passing ships,
    they know your worth—
        it's still the loneliest place
           on earth.

Oo

The Great Lakes abound with rocky reefs and shallow-water shoals that have destroyed many ships. Lighthouses in these remote waters need to withstand winter storms that pound the structures with huge waves and sheets of ice.

New building techniques allowed construction of lighthouses on treacherous places like Spectacle Reef in Lake Huron, where a lighthouse was completed in 1874. Its chief engineer brought the same crew and special equipment to Lake Superior to build a lighthouse on Stannard Rock (1883).

Only single men served on offshore lights. Harsh conditions and isolation made these stations physically and mentally demanding for the keepers who often stayed on duty throughout the eight-month shipping season. In 1926 bad weather on Lake Superior delayed a supply ship bound for the Rock of Ages Light. By the time the ship arrived the keepers were down to their last can of tomatoes.

It's no wonder that keepers at Stannard Rock, over 20 miles from the nearest land, dubbed it "the loneliest place in the world."

Pp

P is for Preservation

Thanks to the efforts
of a few,
lights rise again
and shine anew.

Lighthouses are in jeopardy. Those that have been taken out of service may be torn down or damaged by weather, erosion, and vandalism. The Coast Guard maintains lights in use for navigation but does not have the resources to restore and preserve historic buildings. The National Historical Lighthouse Preservation Act of 2000 allows the Coast Guard to transfer ownership, at no cost, to preservation groups.

The good news is that lighthouses have friends. History buffs, youth groups, and lighthouse organizations have stepped up to save the lights. The Great Lakes Lighthouse Keepers Association began to restore the St. Helena Island Light on Lake Michigan in 1986. Over the years the association has brought new life to many other lights on the Great Lakes.

While their original purpose may be obsolete, lighthouses are more popular than ever. Restored lights and lighthouse museums encourage interest in historic heritage and bring tourists and money into local communities.

Running a lighthouse was often a family affair. Lighthouses came with free living quarters to encourage keepers to have their families with them.

In remote stations without electricity, running water, or easy access to a town, families needed to be self-sufficient. Children helped their parents with gardening, raising animals, and maintaining the station. The lighthouse and living quarters had to be kept shipshape for surprise inspections from the district supervisor. If they weren't boarded or homeschooled, lighthouse children often had to walk or row many miles to school. At the Sackets Harbor Light, also known as Horse Island Light on Lake Ontario, the Ward children went to school in the winter only when they could walk safely across the ice.

You can visit many lighthouse quarters that have been restored and opened to the public like those at the Charlotte-Genesee Lighthouse on Lake Ontario or the Seul Choix Point Light on Lake Michigan.

Q is for Quarters

Help Mum and Dad
with endless chores,
but run free once
you're out of doors.

R r

Lighthouse keepers often risked their lives to rescue sailors and passengers from sinking ships. The Rock of Ages Light, on Lake Superior, lived up to its name in 1933. The steamer *Cox* ran aground on a reef near the light. The keepers rescued all 125 passengers and crew who huddled on the stairs in the light tower until help came the next day.

Beginning in 1876 the United States Life-Saving Service established over 60 lifesaving stations on the Great Lakes, most near a lighthouse. The crews, known as *surfmen*, were trained in beach rescue. They used boats and special devices like the Lyle gun, which fired a lifesaving line to those in distress.

One of the first stations was on Lake Michigan at the Point Betsie Lighthouse near Frankfort. In 1880 the schooner *J.H. Hartzell* ran aground at the foot of a bluff 10 miles down the coast. In bitter wind and snow the surfmen dragged rescue equipment to the wreck and saved the crew from where they clung to the rigging of the sinking ship.

R is for Rescue

The crew clings
to the frozen mast.
The brave surfmen
are here at last!

S is for Straits of Mackinac

We watch the sunrise,
gazing in awe
over the Straits of Mackinac.

The Straits of Mackinac connect Lakes Huron and Michigan at their northern ends. This narrow stretch of water is buffeted by treacherous winds, strong currents, and filled with shallows and rocky reefs. The straits are a major shipping lane and one of the most dangerous areas on the Lakes.

The Old Mackinac Point Light, built like a limestone castle, guided ships moving through the narrowest point in the straits. In 1957 a new five-mile-long suspension bridge, known as the "Mighty Mac," opened, illuminating the straits at night and making the lighthouse obsolete.

Featured in the romantic film *Somewhere in Time*, the Round Island Light guided vessels heading for the booming summer resort at Mackinac Island. Abandoned in 1947 the light deteriorated through storms and vandalism until it was near collapse. The Great Lakes Lighthouse Keepers Association and Boy Scout Troop 323, along with other local and federal groups, began to restore the light and relit it in 1996.

S s

T is for Tower

Big or little,
short or tall,
a good ship captain
knows them all.

Most people picture a lighthouse as a white tower topped by a beam, like the one at Pointe aux Barques on Lake Huron. But there are other types and styles of lighthouses. A square tower sticking out of the lakeside roof of the house identifies the schoolhouse style like the Stony Point (Henderson) Light on Lake Ontario. There are also skeletal steel towers such as the Alpena Light (on Huron); pyramidal styles, such as the Presque Isle North Pierhead Light (on Erie); octagonal, such as the Milwaukee North Point Light (on Michigan); and the square design of lights like Copper Harbor (on Superior).

Lights tend to be constructed of local materials, wood, stone, and brick. In some instances, like Big Sable Point, crumbling towers have been encased in steel or iron plates to stabilize them.

Not all lights were towers. Ships with beacons on the masts marked offshore hazards where building a permanent lighthouse was too difficult. The last lightship on the lakes, the United States lightship *Huron* guided vessels around shoals for nearly 50 years. It now serves as a museum in Port Huron, Michigan.

Early lighthouse keepers of the United States Lighthouse Establishment were civilian political appointees often with poor qualifications for the position. In the mid-1850s the newly created Lighthouse Board established stricter rules and standards governing lighthouses. Keepers needed to be able to read and write, as well as have some skill at mathematics and boating. Along with new regulations came better training, equipment, and support. To encourage reading, the Board distributed portable libraries of about 50 books, moving them every few months among the light stations.

In 1939 President Franklin Roosevelt merged the existing lighthouse agency with the U.S. Coast Guard. The Coast Guard rebuilt many stations and deactivated others. Today the U.S. Coast Guard Ninth District maintains the lights of the Great Lakes, proudly carrying out its mission to help those in peril on the seas. The Coast Guard works with civilian lighthouse organizations to turn the historic structures over to a new generation of keepers.

U is for U. S. Coast Guard

Whatever the need,
whatever it takes,
the U.S. Coast Guard
protects the lakes.

U
u

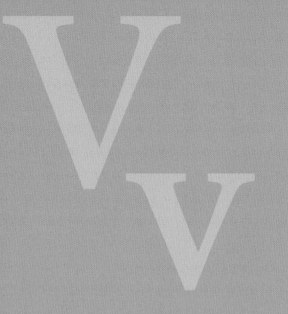

Dream of living in a lighthouse? You can live that dream. From rustic to refined there's a lighthouse experience for you. Lighthouse tourism is booming. Take a lighthouse tour or cruise, or stay in a lighthouse on your next shore vacation.

As a volunteer keeper you can experience the romance and solitude of lighthouse life while contributing to historic preservation. Volunteers at the St. Helena Island Light on Lake Michigan live and work at the light as the keepers did 100 years ago without water or electricity. Some lighthouses require volunteers to bring their R.V. or camper, while others provide living quarters with modern conveniences. Volunteer keepers assist with greeting visitors, providing historic information, and doing chores suited to their abilities.

For those who require more comforts there are lighthouses converted into bed-and-breakfast inns. The Sand Hills Lighthouse on Lake Superior and the Braddock Point Lighthouse on Lake Ontario feature elegant Victorian interiors along with a tranquil stay.

V is for Visit and Volunteer

Lighthouse life
gives you the chance
to know excitement
and romance.

W is for Women

They faced the risks,
the solitude,
and toiled with quiet
fortitude.

Lighthouses thrived at a time when rough work was considered suitable only for men. But a number of women were keepers at Great Lakes lights.

Rachel Wolcott, the first woman to serve as a keeper on the Great Lakes, got the job the way most women did then. She took over the Marblehead Light on Lake Erie in 1832 when her husband, the light keeper, died. Already in place and familiar with the operation of the light, wives, and sometimes daughters, could step into positions that were often hard to fill.

Harriet Colfax, whose prior qualifications consisted of teaching voice and piano in upstate New York, became the keeper of the Old Michigan City Light in 1861. She kept the light for 43 years. Her diligence and kindness became a legend to mariners on Lake Michigan who referred to the light as "Miss Harriet's."

The good news for the ladies who kept the lights: they got the same pay as the men.

W
W

X Marks the Spot

Battered by
the wind and waves,
strong ships go down
to silent graves.

When a fierce snow squall swept Lake Superior in November 1975, the freighter *Edmund Fitzgerald*, its 26 tons of iron ore, and all 29 crew members vanished. Heading toward Whitefish Bay for safety, Captain Ernest M. McSorley radioed that the ship was taking on heavy seas but added, "We are holding our own." That was his last communication.

The Whitefish Point Light Station marks the entrance to the shelter of Whitefish Bay. On that stormy night in 1975 the lighthouse went dark due to a power outage. The area around Whitefish Point is called Shipwreck Coast and the light station now hosts the Great Lakes Shipwreck Museum.

An estimated 6,000 ships have gone down in the Great Lakes, claiming more than 30,000 lives. Underwater exploration continues to uncover wrecks of lost ships. You don't have to be a diver to see historical wrecks. Glass-bottom boats offer tours of the Thunder Bay National Marine Sanctuary in northern Lake Huron to see some of the 116 known wrecks.

Lighthouses were once necessary for guiding ships. However, the Global Positioning System (GPS), modern optics, and navigational technologies have made the traditional lighthouse and its keeper obsolete. Automation of lighthouses began with the invention of a sun valve, which turned the beacon on and off with the rising and setting of the sun. The Baileys Harbor Range Lights on Lake Michigan were the first to be automated in 1923. Astronomical clocks, radio beacons, and other devices allowed remote operation of light stations.

Lighthouses converted to electrical power as electrical networks crossed the country. By the 1960s all but a few of the Great Lakes lighthouses had been automated. Sherwood Point Lighthouse on Lake Michigan, automated in 1983, was the last manned light on the American side of the Great Lakes.

But technology has not changed the affection people have for lighthouses. Lighthouses offer a connection to our past, a symbol of dedication and duty that never becomes obsolete.

Yy

Y is for Yesterday

Electric power
and automation
replaced a keeper's
dedication.

Known as the Zenith City, Duluth, Minnesota, sits at the western end of Lake Superior, 2,300 miles from the Atlantic Ocean. In the mid-1800s Duluth became a primary hub for the transportation of ore, grain, and other products from America's Heartland to the Atlantic.

Duluth's Breakwater Lights protect Duluth's ship canal: one on the north pier and the other two on the south breakwater. Within walking distance of one another, the lighthouses show three distinct types of lights—conical, skeletal, and square.

The Duluth harbor is infamous for its heavy fogs. Bells, whistles, and a diaphone foghorn with its familiar mournful *bee-oh* call were used in the port over the years to warn off ships. The citizens of Duluth often complained about the noise. But when an electric signal replaced the foghorn in 1968, many missed the sound that had echoed through the city for generations. The horn was reactivated in 1995 but a few years later the last officially operating foghorn in North America was silenced.

Z is for Zenith City

The foghorn echoes
throughout the bay
to show each ship
the safest way.

For Audrey Macks Mitnick
— Helen

For Kathy Tank and the Port Washington Lighthouses
— Renée

Sleeping Bear Press

2395 South Huron Parkway, Suite 200
Ann Arbor, MI 48104
www.sleepingbearpress.com

Printed and bound in the United States.

Library of Congress Cataloging-in-Publication Data

Wilbur, Helen L., 1948-
B is for beacon : a Great Lakes lighthouse alphabet / written by Helen
L. Wilbur ; illustrated by Renée Graef.
pages cm
Summary: "Following the alphabet this book uses poetry and expository
text to explore the history of lighthouses on the Great Lakes, detailing
famous structures, local lore, as well as notable moments in Great Lakes
history"--Provided by the publisher.
Audience: Ages 6-10.
ISBN 978-1-58536-916-4
1. Lighthouses--Great Lakes (North America)--History--Juvenile works.
2. Alphabet books--Juvenile works. I. Graef, Renee, illustrator. II.
Title. III. Title: Great Lakes lighthouse alphabet.
VK1023.3.W55 2016
386'.8550977--dc23
2015027633